The Refugee Camp

For Richard —

Here's an account of my days as a spy. (Have they ever ended?) I'm still a refugee, of course. Thank you for helping me with the sequence when I first started working on it, for taking "Crossing the Border" for <u>Western Humanities Review</u>, and for choosing the book for the Paris Review Prize — even though Zoo Press soon went ingloriously out of business. My admiration and gratitude are boundless.

Ever the best of friends,
always your pupil,

John

11/3/2011

The Refugee Camp

John Drury

Turning Point Books

© 2011 by John Philip Drury

Published by Turning Point Books
P.O. Box 541106
Cincinnati, OH 45254-1106

ISBN: 9781936370498
LCCN: 2011938084

Poetry Editor: Kevin Walzer
Business Editor: Lori Jareo

Cover art: "Melancholia," Albrecht Dürer (1471-1528)

Visit us on the web at www.turningpointbooks.com

Acknowledgments

Thanks to the editors of the following periodicals for publishing poems that appear in this book:

Another Chicago Magazine: section 26 of "The Refugee Camp" (titled "Under the Imperial Eagle")
The Blue Writer: section 44 of "The Refugee Camp" (titled "Liaison Office")
The Journal: section 47 of "The Refugee Camp" (titled "Weather Report")
The Literary Review: section 36 of "The Refugee Camp" (titled "Applying for Asylum")
Open Places: "The Refugee Camp" (sections 1-5, 7, 9-12, 14-17, 23, 28-29, 31-34, 37-38, 40-43, 45-46, and 48)
Pequod: sections 13 and 39 of "The Refugee Camp" (titled "The Agency Mural" and "The Double Spires")
River Styx: sections 6 and 35 of "The Refugee Camp" (titled "Interrupted Song" and "The Slopes")
Western Humanities Review: "Crossing the Border"

I'm grateful to the Charles Phelps Taft Memorial Fund of the University of Cincinnati, the Ohio Arts Council, and the Ingram Merrill Foundation for grants that helped me complete this book. I also want to thank Richard Howard for his advice and encouragement, Pat Mora for her suggestions, and Dennis Evanosky, John Keeler, Fritz Keppler, Jim Linn, Dail Mahood Richie, Rick Rowan, Pete Steiner, and especially John and Jean Walker for their friendship while I was living in Germany.

for LaWanda Walters

amor mi mosse, che mi fa parlare

.

Table of Contents

Time: 1972
Place: West Germany

Ich sitze am Strassenhang.
Der Fahrer wechselt das Rad.
Ich bin nicht gern, wo ich herkomme.
Ich bin nicht gern, wo ich hinfahre.
Warum sehe ich den Radwechsel
Mit Ungeduld?

—Bertolt Brecht

These Strangers, in a foreign World,
Protection asked of me—
Befriend them, lest Yourself in Heaven
Be found a Refugee—

—Emily Dickinson

The real interrogator is a voice within.

—Yusef Komunyakaa

The Refugee Camp

The Refugee Camp

1.

In the ruined city
of toymakers and singing guilds,
they were so fanatical at the war's end
even civilians fought,
shooting from rubble, from cellar windows.

I climb the cobbled streets
to Heathen's Tower
past half-timbered houses and the repaired
wreckage of air strikes, patchworks
of clean and weathered quarrystone.

When I say to a friend, *Too bad
we bombed the churches,*
he corrects me:
the Nazis used them
to quarter the Gestapo.

And yet—a song remains,
if only a clashing music,
as trams wrench
around tight corners, whining
as power lines spark, in Nuremberg.

2.

Each morning I trudge uphill
to the refugee camp where I work.
Aliens huddle by the vestibule
while officials brush past,
muttering a password
to the guard at a glassed-in booth
who buzzes them—and me—
through the heavy door.
Turned back, the refugees grumble and curse,
kick cinders in the parking lot.

Everyone says they carry knives,
hands jammed in pockets,
their faces half scraped, half stubble,
women left behind
in cramped flats or muddy villages.
They stare at our questionnaires
and leave too many blanks.
I learn *Do you know nothing, sir?*
and *See you later, mister*
in languages I will never begin to fathom.

3.

How fitting that the camp
borders the old imperial city,
once a crossroads, a stopping point
on the treacherous, overland trade route
to Venice and the orient.

How fitting that the patron saint,
a hermit named Sebaldus,
lived in the forest
and turned icicles to firewood,
his tomb lifted up by carved snails.

How fitting that, in the stadium,
rallies arose like architecture:
pillars of light, brass bands
and brown-shirted blocks, a cobblestone
courtyard of helmets.

How fitting, too, that the burghers
who smeared a silver cross
with paint, to fool looters in the Middle Ages,
passed on their nickname:
"Blackeners of God."

4.

From the castle, walk down
past the knight with his heels on a dragon,
past the woodwork and bull's eye glass of Dürer's house,
past the antique shops, dark with Menorahs,
past the town hall's dungeons,
past the golden fountain, with Moses near the top,
past the young albino caning a chair,
past the baker pressing almonds into gingerbread,
past the stone ox alongside the Meat Bridge,
past the restaurant over the river.

Turn right at the green-gold spires of St. Lawrence
and loiter by tables of campaign leaflets
and clusters of burghers debating,
poking fingers in the air,
by the ancient men with one leg, or one arm,
asleep in wheelchairs, heads back in the sun,
by bitter-faced crones in black shawls,
by piles of coins, shining between empty trousers,
by a man with five watches on his wrist,
by a blind man playing an accordion.

5.

Praise to the chamber music
in the castle of Frederick Barbarossa.

Praise to Dürer's last journey
to the North Sea, to sketch a beached whale.

Praise to the organist in the loft
retracing her steps, her intricate pedalwork.

Praise to the cobbler who mends cracked heels
and reinforces eyelets in a boot.

Praise to the tankards and cut-glass bowls,
to the breakfast beer and blue trout.

Praise to the robber knight whose horse
leapt the wall, whose hoofmarks are nicked in stone.

Praise to David, the apprentice, who knows
the gleaming-thread melody and how to trim leather.

Praise to my attic room, and the bathtub downstairs
that empties on the floor of the cellar.

Praise to the woman dentist I greet on the stairs
and the padded chair I glimpse on my way up.

Praise to macaroons and hot blueberry wine,
to the walled city, to tunnels with deep-set skylights.

6.

In Nuremberg, the burghers roar
    at football matches. Rowers,
banned from the river, glide beyond
    stone walls, the moat, the towers.

Mid-afternoon, an old man and a child hunch over a
chessboard in a sausage parlor. The waitress, puffy in a
dirndl, polishes glasses and arranges them on a tray.
The game could go on forever, and she'd never hurry
them to leave. Through the window, I see a plaque of
sunlight, a bit crooked, on a rebuilt house with a red-
tiled roof. In the open doorway, a basket flashes.

A surge of tourist groups outflanks
    the marketplace's flowers
and watercolors that depict
    stone walls, the moat, the towers.

Lugging a pillowcase of laundry, I pass a stucco
cottage with a low wall. A woman bashes green bottles
with a hammer. I nearly stop and gape, astounded by
relentless smashing, a rain of slivers, a sprinkle of glass
bits. Then I go on, still hearing chimes, but looking,
instead, at flowerbeds, ivy trained up a wall, a mattress
airing out on a windowsill.

The pictures offer pleasantness—
    nothing about the powers
of darkness—while floodlights overwhelm
    stone walls, the moat, the towers.

7.

The music of the future
stirred in these streets.
Wagner, the composer and rabble-rouser
who signaled to rebels
from a lookout tower in 1849,
tricked a carpenter at a beer house
into singing at midnight, raising a commotion
that spread to the streets then
vanished. He laughed
as he strolled on deserted
moonlit alleys of the old walled city:
all changed in his opera
to a scene with Beckmesser, marker of errors.
At night, when I hug the wall
called *Frauentor Mauer*, I watch from the shadows
as women lean out, the light from their windows
dropping on men pacing like watchdogs.
A brunette in red, with freckles on her breasts,
cocks her head and coos "Schatzi, Schatzi,"
and I enter into the light.

8.

They battle in taverns, defending their beers
and their accents. They howl in the streets
at midnight, heroic tenors
in an endless beggar's opera.

Cowering, they wait for
blows, vouchers, asylum,
in the corridors of the agency
where mops stew in buckets.

After work, in Tengelmann's grocery store,
they puzzle over the piles of wurst,
sliced and stacked like old vinyl records,
and head back to the camp with red plastic satchels.

At the agency, one of them tugs
my sleeve and whispers, "Be careful
of the man at the gate, very."
Another asks, "Is it permitted to fume here?"

Another offers to sell me
an enormous radio—"not stolen."
Another returns his questionnaire
slashed with an X.

9.

Morning lights up
my room, and so I go forth
riding the streetcars, climbing steep lanes,
crossing the Hangman's Bridge
halfway to the former hospice for incurables.

And so I look up
at the twisty weathervanes
and the windowboxes of petunias, and down
to the cages of fish in the river,
and the drainspouts, and a skiff drifting under an arch.

And so I slow down
in the shadow of St. Sebaldus,
where Jesus crumbles beneath his crumbling lumber,
and eyes that weep crumble,
and rain rounds the angles of sandstone.

And so I come home
to a room with a slanting ceiling,
and wallpaper patterned like a rebus,
and a faucet that drips on porcelain, almost a motet,
and a window that funnels in quiet light.

10.

A drunken bagpiper woke up
on a cart piled with corpses
during the plague and started
to play. Drunkenness
blesses: he was saved
by smoked beer. As I zig-zag
up twisting lanes, leaving
the *Dudelsack* fountain,
the piper squeezes his bag
as if throttling a goose.

I think of the drunken brawl
set off by Beckmesser's howling,
his futile serenade
in quest of impossible love.
I think of that harmony
in discord, and how false
it now seems, though beautiful.
I think of the sudden dispersal
of the crowd, and how true
the stillness, though beautiful.

11.

On the mirror I have taped
postcards of engravings:
St. Jerome and *Melancholia*.
I admire the lion
in the Renaissance chamber—
and the muscular, disgruntled angel
in the open air.
Some evenings, after work,
I pull *The Cantos* or *Far
from the Madding Crowd* off the desk
that closes up into itself
and listen to "ear, ear
for the sea-surge" or Gabriel Oak
feeling the earth, under stars, revolving.
Some evenings, I look away
from the portable typewriter
and the packets of pale stationery
and the picture of tools and implements
unlit by the sun—rising or setting—
that strikes me, now, as a hub with broken spokes.

12.

The world was created
from parchment, wood, and mucilage

when Martin Behaim, newly knighted, returned
from voyages down the Ivory Coast,

boasting of discoveries, adding a mythical
Isle of Seven Cities to the North Atlantic,

and Glockenthon painted the known
and imaginary world of mermaids and flags,

miniature elephants, kings and saints,
and a zodiac girdling the ecliptic

in *Nourenberc*, the "rocky mountain,"
where the rock is sandstone, quarried near the castle.

I like to imagine them, painter and navigator,
cutting the gores of the map

with barber's shears, then gluing
their handiwork, loose as paper dolls,

to the "earth apple," fussing
over the gaps and wedges at the poles

but pleased with the skull cap they paste
to the top: an angel like a bird of prey.

13.

Bastion on a hilltop, the complex dominates the valley
where I dawdle on my way to work. Office, oasis—
our suite in a German agency, haven for refugees,
chain gates partway open, fastened to the hill by the
dead weight of files. The pink and grey exterior bears
an abstract triangle of horse heads, birds emerging
from crescents, fish at the bottom.

War, here, is the contingency. We'd fall immediately,
sparing others who'd flee to tunnels and bunkers in
the western mountains. Our liaison office—scene of
liaisons on the couch, brandy and scotch in a cabinet,
next door to the U.N. reps ("Don't trust them"), a
floor above philanthropic foundations, below a West
German intelligence outpost—welcomes the aliens,
outcasts, runaways, pumping them for information of
military value. ("Don't trust them either.")

Whenever we confer, the radio booms out polkas to
muffle what we say, confidences or passing remarks.
("Upstairs, they listen in.") And some things ("we're
bugged") can't bear discussion, but must be scribbled
on slips of paper, then burned in the ashtray. And
nothing whatsoever on the telephone, instrument of
deceit, conduit of spies.

Every day we burn our messages, pack up carbons
into parcels for shredding at headquarters—in the
name of the mission, and the code of conduct, and
the security clearance.

14.

In the dimming light of autumn,
as work lets out early,

I cross the highway and head
down the footpath toward a bridge.

To my right, through woods, a stream wanders off;
to my left, garden plots still blossom.

I stop at the bridge, looking back up
at the agency building and its towering smokestack.

Sheep tramp over the pathway, green crosses
on the rams' heads, the shepherd

in lederhosen and a waterproof cape,
a boy trailing behind, holding a bottle of Afri-Cola.

A refugee halts beside me and points
at blotches, purple and smeared. Berry stains.

"Look," he says, "blood." He grabs my sleeve
and waves at a zig-zag trail down the path.

"Look, how he couldn't walk straight,
how he must have been suffering.

"There he leaned on a gate to rest.
Look at it. There it is. Blood."

15.

Everyone looks rattled:
an engineer from Cairo
who scrubs kettles
in the mess hall of an American base;
a Polish architect
who tries to supervise the carpenters
remodeling the police bureau
though they shake their hammers at him;
a death camp survivor
who hated Russia
and didn't like Israel
and doesn't care for Germany
and trembles as he holds a notice;
a Rumanian teenager
who hangs around the compound
in a U.S. Army field jacket
but has to surrender it
to the silver-haired, gangly
liaison officer
who pats him on the back as he takes it.

.

16.

What do you know?
I am here where
  the rail lines intersect
    and the moat is preserved
for strollers, where the old walls are thick.
  I have kept to myself—
    awake in a cot
with a thin wool blanket,
  asleep in a ditch,
    in a great observatory.

What led you here?
I could say the pole star,
  or a faded map.
    I could also say "hope"
or confess "no home."
  But for now I climb up
    to a lofty bunk, and a metal tray
with compartments, and a mended shirt,
  and a wristwatch ticking
    with a cracked face.

17.

In the church of St. Lawrence
a bearded elf, clutching a mallet,
crouches beneath a stone tower.
It's the sculptor himself, Adam Kraft.

Above him, the saint it was carved for
handles a gridiron, smiling as if
he knew something. He carries,
like everyone, his own undoing.

When the Roman authorities
coveted the church's wealth, and taxed it,
he doled out its money
and presented a ragged mob, his only riches.

The story goes: when he'd roasted
on the grate for an hour
he told the executioner
Turn me over, I'm done on that side.

In memory, the cooks here in Nuremberg
grill fingers of bratwurst
over beechwood coals and serve them
on heart-shaped pewter.

18.

Always the clattering of boxcars, traffic
over switches, always the hooting in the night.

I lie in bed, listening for the clang
of a warning gate in the distance, thinking

of overhead wires, a musical staff of current
near my dormer window. I bumble into sleep.

And rise just before the alarm goes off:
a broken clock that's stuck on the same wake-up time.

And then the rituals of rising and departing,
a whore's bath at the sink, my consultations

of the mirror, its brown edges like a letter
charred in a fire. I drip on a towel—

until it bunches beneath my feet—and then
on the wavy linoleum. I brew tea

in tapwater, never hot enough, and try to stir
away the clouds, surrounded by vanity mirrors.

Below my shuttered window, a street-washing truck
shuffles by, buffing the gutter. When I open the latches

on the gray day, I see a gray dog
lapping a puddle of soapy water.

19.

Cheered on by the radio,
an American expatriate
singing "Hallo partner, danke schön,"
I venture one evening to a Kontakt meeting.

But the Bierstube where we gather,
with a bust of Dürer
on the mantel below some antlers,
doesn't loosen me up.

I shift between two conversations,
both in slangy English, and shift
in my chair, the varnish worn through at the top,
letting the brew fizzle.

Contact is what I crave, of course,
but I must look ravenous—
or perhaps not interested at all.
We leave in a clumsy group,

tumbling onto the bumpy street
where a trio links arms and skips
toward a lamp post, singing "All I want
is a room somewhere."

20.

I learn to sharpen my pencils
with a razor blade and take up sketching,
hesitantly at first, remaining indoors
and drawing pine cones, bananas, my left hand.
Eventually, I take to the streets, pausing
in front of a pet shop to sketch budgies,
asleep or ruffling their wings.
I find swans in a park and sketch them
in a lined pocket notebook, loose-leaf
so I can toss out what I botch.

I fancy that I'm learning to see.
And I find it's a give and take
with the immediate world.
Under a shade tree, I sketch a boy
in his scout uniform, a waitress with a platter,
a steeple rising through leaves.
I keep going, even though an old man peers
at my drawing of a half-timbered gable
and mutters "Nicht gut" and shuffles away
from the airy spaces, the roof left hanging.

21.

On a ledge, the prince of this world
displays the finery of his costume
while worms and snakes devour his back.
Perhaps he's a merchant, wealthy
from the wool trade or the tanning of hides.

He keeps an elaborate beer stein
at one of the taverns—Glass Heaven or Sea of Planks—
and wears a morning coat with an ermine collar
and possesses the pawned crown
of the emperor Sigismund.

In time of war, he serves as a street captain,
inspecting the watch guards, dispatching patrols.
Presiding as a magistrate, he condemns a baker
whose rolls are too small to be locked
in an iron cage and immersed in the river.

We know him as we know the monastic knights
from their oath shields, as we know
Peter Vischer from the bronze self-portrait he cast:
square-jawed, wearing an apron,
raising a small testing hammer.

22.

It's a saying that's printed on beer steins and post cards, a drinking jingle perhaps, or a civic motto:

> Nuremberg's golden funnel is said
> To make men wise and clear the head.

In a café window, dolls enact the story: a teacher, dressed in a robe with a white ruff, pours the contents of a green bottle through a funnel into a dunce's head. Why liqueur soaking his brains would help is beyond me. Flasks are for sale, with miniature funnels rubber-banded to the necks.

It seems good natured, a municipal jest. And yet this free imperial city, this bottleneck, this locus of towers and mastersongs, this walled town severed by a river, this hive of medieval craftsmen funneled a parade of stormtroopers through its twisting, cobbled lanes.

As pedestrians pour through the underpass, a woman on her hands and knees rubs chalk on a half finished portrait—a madonna whose knowing child will be trampled when the artist goes home.

But for now, at least, she's captured the edge of a smile, and with dull pastels a light reflected in the eyes.

For now, it carols into focus.

23.

After rondos on a forte-piano
in the gallery, I walk
through the fortified town, in the shadows
of the custom house, over the Pegnitz,

another night wanderer
below the leaded windowpanes
that throw a brilliant quilt of light
on the sloping street.

Much has risen from a jumble
of stones, but not the quaint house
that belonged to Hans Sachs.
It is not, any more, his town,

though his statue presides
over Volvos and Volkswagen beetles,
his hammer above the workbench—
of course, it is lifted to strike.

I look for a fork of lightning—
but the sky's blank, the wind's as baffled as I am,
and I backtrack my way through the city,
another night wanderer.

24.

One afternoon on the way home,
downhill on an asphalt path through a field

by garden plots with shacks and trellises,
I pass two cyclists crossing the bridge.

Nearly to the stand of trees where a fence
encloses some machinery, I hear a crash

and look back. One of the riders, a girl,
lies motionless on the concrete.

I want to run there and help, but I stare.
I want to call "Are you OK?" in German,

but I can't puzzle out the idiom. The front wheel,
spinning in the air, flashes a bit of sunlight

from the spokes, but I stay put, unable to budge,
my feet as heavy as buckets of paving stones.

The other cyclist walks her bike back to the bridge
and leans over her companion, who hasn't moved.

At last—and suddenly—she rises and mounts her bike,
wobbly at first but straightening, pedaling uphill. At last,

I turn and continue, troubled more for myself
than for anyone who's fallen down and risen.

25.

In a blocked-off street, campaign fliers
piled in a stroller, I notice
a woman behind the Young Socialist table
fronted by a banner with a rose.
She listens to her comrades
arguing with passersby but says nothing,
just a widening smile as she glances across the street.
I'm smitten with her eyes that squint
because of the sunlight, her arms around herself,
her body shaking to ward off the November wind
that burns her freckled cheeks, a scarf
above her fringe of auburn hair.
When she packs up to leave, she places
a long-stemmed rose, displayed on the table,
in her satchel, cocks her head, and looks in my direction.
And though I get up the nerve to walk by,
I lower my gaze and continue to the tram stop.
Waiting, I see her board a streetcar
headed in the opposite direction.
She smiles my way and vanishes.

26.

I know about the rally grounds from seeing *Triumph
of the Will* in German class, but the park and pleasure
boats surprise me. Swans feed in the marsh grass of
Silver Lake, formed when the bulldozed land for a
stadium to hold half a million party members filled
with rainwater. Now there's a sign, with a white skull
where someone's etched a smile, warning of mortal
danger from hydrogen sulfide. A cauldron of turbu-
lence bubbles near the freshly mown lawn of the
shore.

90% of the walled city was destroyed by air strikes, yet
somebody still had to scrub away swastikas from
official buildings, occupied by the invaders. It's hard
to imagine the rubble I see in the grainy photograph.
The Allies, billeted in a hotel near the railway station,
sent out teams to disinfect and fumigate and exter-
minate vermin and control the black market.

The Nazis had it coming, sure, but where does that
leave us now? Soldiers in their "street cruisers" blast
through the shuttered dorfs, electric guitars from
Armed Forces Radio piercing through to a room
where a child feels out a Bach invention. His sister,
gussied up and snapping her gum, sashays down the
street, swinging a transistor radio, heading toward GIs
outside the commissary. Their mother, who barely re-
members the war, daydreams over a bestseller, the
light from a fringed lamp turning the pages gold.

27.

At the base library,
a rambling wooden temporary building,
I run into Smitty, a classmate from language school.
When I ask about his assignment, he says
"I'm an undercover cop now. Customs.
I bust drug dealers and dumb grunts
who don't know where to hide the stuff.
They can't think of a better place
than under the floorboards. It leaves
a bad taste in my mouth, believe me."

I remember an earlier meeting
when I first arrived in Germany
and was passing through a courtyard
of a Nazi fortification. He wore
the helmet and white gloves
of the Military Police and leered
as he recommended the Eros Center
where women in bras and panties, some in fur coats
or cowgirl get-ups, lounged on carpeted islands in a room
dark and cavernous, like a subway station or a grotto.

28.

"Take place," the little one,
who has studied in London, commands,
so I take a seat
at the party in a purple-walled flat
where I'm the only guest.

There are two of them—
Ulricha, Brigitta—and me.
"Here comes," I think, and gulp
a whiskey sour and choke down
a cracker heaped with caviar.

I'm dying to take place,
or take either of them,
though I've never heard of Smetana
(gurgling on the stereo) and am unimpressed by music
that's nothing but a rivulet swelling to the sea.

After the trams stop running
and I'm still there, they put me on the sofa
and I wait, drunk and wakeful, and rejoice
when one slips by to the bathroom
and hold my breath when she passes, again, not stopping.

29.

The entrails of night—
when the double spires
are encrusted, as if underwater,
barnacled with men
who climb with their fingernails,
clamber over bodies, fall back
to the roof, rise up, lose their grip.
And gold scales fall
to the street, landing on
the circus wagon left there at dusk.

The entries of night—
when the climbing of men on the run,
demanding asylum, jostles
the bells in their yokes
and rattles the pipes
of Pachelbel's voluble organ,
and a tiny Iranian
whose faith embraces all faiths
embraces the cross at the apex
and cannot be unstuck.

30.

Go back to the wall where breath burns,
where women click rings on glass,
each lit window a shrine, and sidle
by the long, curving shadow
from round tower to wide-open gate.

Keep going, down into the moat
overgrown with grasses and wildflowers.
Circle the medieval defenses, cross over the river
on a chain bridge, veering and stumbling
over cobblestones, trying to lose all bearings.

This is the walking tour
omitted by guides, not wandering or sightseeing
but a probing of the spirit, whatever
lies in rubble and scree like a sandstone quarry,
scarred walls of jagged facets.

When the tram delivers you
to your cool room, your bed of three cushions,
let the comforter swallow you whole,
a recurrent dream of walls, steep curving walls
that force you inward.

31.

In the general assembly
of the theatre, Bauhaus-modern
but seedy, we take in the pink flesh
of blue movies. All foreigners here,

the sexual small talk
defeats us, the whips
and ticklers of insinuation
in the dubbed, detached voices.

We laugh at the hottest parts,
hush up when jokes are consummated,
clap and hoot when the film
breaks to a white glare.

None of us diplomats,
we slouch in plush, gouged chairs
and let the warm tones overcome us,
our dark inquiring faces

rouged and lipsticked and mascaraed
by the flash of rousing flesh,
by the mouth's own opus of attention,
by the close-ups of opening.

32.

But where's the retreat
into fantasy, where's the relief?
All we see in the movie
are dingy tints, the flesh tones
bleeding along the edges, a port-wine stain
on the film itself. When the stars couple,
a poodle cowers under the daybed.
When they finish, a white-gloved hand
proffers a magnum of champagne
and searches the pants crumpled on a stool
for a wallet. Where's the refuge
if not in the dark, if not
in the spectacle of sex?
—I think of the artisans
on display in the *Waffenhof*,
a courtyard within the city walls
where baskets are woven, vases blown,
pottery spun on a wheel, horseshoes
hammered and, molten, bent around a spike.
It is real and it is not.

33.

In the Middle Ages
a coppersmith, painted red,
rode to the parish fairs,
smearing pedestrians with "blood."

No games like *that* anymore,
except in the special effects of movies.
On the river, the Pegnitz,
beside the thick walls

where the bars of a portcullis
were lowered in wartime,
fishermen costumed in cone-shaped hats
battled each other with pikes.

Children pummeled grown-ups for money
on *Peppering Day*, but flailed
against doors and latched shutters
on *Knocker's Night* for free.

Cutlers danced with their sabres.
Butchers paraded with a quarter-ton sausage.
A stage on wheels, called *Hell*,
had to be stormed and demolished.

34.

Toys are everywhere:
flat tin soldiers, a two-dimensional band

with cymbals, drums, trombones,
a crèche scene with palm trees and camels.

The city prides itself
on its trifles. Everywhere I see

the image of a caravan of wagons
moving these playthings through the world.

My favorite toy is the professor
with a butterfly net in a three-wheeled cart,

but I also like the tin automobile
with the caption *To the Pole*—

Amundsen, his coat as thick as a bear suit,
sitting under an umbrella

that is half of a globe: yellow Greenland,
pink Canada, green Scandinavia.

Some of the playthings are edible:
prune men with walnut heads.

But their buttons are tinfoil, their helmets felt,
the foam on their beer steins cotton.

35.

In a house, baroque and spared from air raids, I dally
by a canvas of a poet on Parnassus, scribbling in the
cold, his winged horse grazing, the muse asleep.

Nearly obscured in the dark aisle of a junk shop, a
bald man arranges a line of spiked helmets.

Carpenters hammer in the market square, putting to-
gether numbered booths, rigging up red and white
canopies.

God of spies, what have I done to unbecome myself?

All over town, on the gates of military posts taken
over by Americans, the imperial eagle clutches a
wreath around a scoured disk of stone.

The world of sandstone crumbles, whether or not a
bombardier fixed it on his cross.

36.

Note how a man walks carefully
on pebbles by the roadside, trying to coax
the soles of his second-hand shoes to last longer.
Note how the benches in a terminal feel softer
than the stares of passing passengers
who pull their luggage on wheels behind them.
Note how the stories about fruit trees,
blossoming on a pool's bank, refresh more
than the lost oasis ever will.
Note how some nights, the headlights
of trucks jab like charging horns
just before the bull gores the befuddled matador,
how some nights, an angel with two swords—
or two crutches—approaches without expression.
Note how random shots after midnight
give way to the shrapnel of dreams in the morning.
Note how security forces
strap on their helmets, their bullet-proof vests,
their holsters, their extra clips,
how even the police dogs wear gas masks.

37.

In the graveyard where Dürer is buried,
the tombstones rise from the ground
like stone couches—positioned
so that boars couldn't dig up the bodies.

Shuffling through dossiers, what
am I digging for? Border guards
mapping their barracks, measuring compounds
and barbed wire, naming each dog in the kennel?

Thinly disguised in mufti, I try
to act natural, always forgetting to air out
my herringbone suit. Our chief tells a courier
"He's a good boy, but green."

I joined to learn German,
which I still haven't mastered,
mumbling and sputtering
and smiling as I listen, as if I understood.

At the corner, an American tank clanks by,
jeeps blare and peel off
with a shriek of tires: an occupation
I'm part of, but don't belong to.

38.

This holy ground, the church of Our Lady,
where painted figures circle, bowing
to the emperor as a glockenspiel chimes,
was the site of the synagogue, razed
a century before the height of the mastersingers.

The plaza before the church
where farmwomen in scarves sell flowers,
where booths are erected for the Christ Child Market,
where merchants display white dresses,
marked the limits of the ghetto in 1349.

Because there was no open area
in the city center, where goods
could be sold "in comfort,"
where tradesmen could barter and loiter,
the houses of Jews were burned down.

In a photograph, the tanks of General Patton
browse in the ruined square
before the ornate façade—the only side standing—
of the bombed-out Frauenkirche.
Nothing has been set right.

39.

I study the corner stonework: a devil, snatching away
a schoolboy who drops his satchel of books, howling
and kicking, not quite repentant that he cheated at
marbles. Another bas-relief makes me frown: a wo-
man throttled with a scarf, as a grosser figure prepares
to strike her. Martyr or miscreant, she does not de-
serve his excesses. I walk around the front of the
church, below the netting that protects the carved
figures, below Eve and Adam and the adamant fig
leaves, below the double spires—one pale green, like
verdigris on brass, one crisscrossed by a gold pattern,
its glittering scales like snakeskin. From the church, a
hymn slips out. When I look inside, the crowd is
meager, seated in chairs at the back, the minister near-
ly whispering from a makeshift altar. I've heard the
great organ before, in the empty nave on a weekday
afternoon, but where is it now? The only accom-
paniment to Luther's chorale likening God to a "stout
castle"—like the burly towers of Nuremberg—is an
organ on wheels. In the hymn, the Almighty is a
"weapon of war." Above the altar, an Annunciation
carved by Veit Stoss, suspended like an elaborate tra-
peze, maintains a constant hush—the instant of
realization. Ahead, someone in a pew, not a celebrant,
focuses a camera.

40.

One day we process
a Bulgarian. Another name
to enter in the green ledger:
"No knowledgeability, not
a prospective source."
Later in the week, someone knifes him
to death in his dormitory bunk.
I walk through the high-ceilinged
hallway, almost choking
on a bucket's disinfectant,
and pick up the dossier on his case.
It doesn't touch me
in the least. I wonder
when I last cried, and remember:
when a bus I was on
didn't stop, and I called out,
and two girls sitting by the exit
laughed at my accent,
and the cut of my jacket,
and the redness darkening my face.

41.

But that humiliation
is nothing, compared to the way

a shopkeeper brandishes
an old broom, flared at the end

and matted with dust puffs,
at a dark-skinned man

in a loose-fitting suit,
all stripes, and a colorful turban;

nothing compared to the welcome
the homeless receive, here to find work

that no one else would put up with,
unschooled in the laws of asylum:

plate scrapers, diggers of mud,
factory drones, crate loaders, scrubwomen;

nothing compared to the blue stare
of functionaries, smirks of cashiers,

where, even if you have enough money,
you're filth, and can never be cleansed,

but you don't have money, or time,
or a way back to a home that never was yours.

42.

In the opera, a poet
wanders into this town
like Kaspar Hauser, same town,
same tune of the prodigy
wild for a muse to tame him.

His song wins the heroine.
Twenty years later
he nurses his *Schnaps*, deals *Skat*,
and wishes he had never peeked
in the church, at the choiring masters.

There he saw her, his Beatrice, his Eva.
He dreams that he wakes
in the Black Forest, under a spruce,
forsaken or simply ignored.
In his prodigal dream, no one bothers him.

Set up as a dyer, he sings for a guild.
The rule-breaker who claimed he was taught
by the birds of the air
has become a stickler, marking
on slates the musical slips of apprentices.

43.

The woman behind a pane
forms words with her lips, blows kisses
to the slowly pacing figures,
some flattened against the stone wall, gawking
at a woman with her bare legs propped up,
working a puzzle. Some of the women
trade gossip and jokes between windows,
pausing to call to the passing men.
Taxis rush by. A police car
idles in front of one entrance.
The black men are greeted
with indifference, or shakes of the head.
In an upper window
an old-timer with frizzy red hair
stares down at the alley's black and white movie.
A man hurries out of one doorway
into the shadows. In the stoop's glow
a blonde steps out, arranging her blouse.
The women in light are still;
the men can't rest in the shadows.

44.

Near closing, when the last piled applications to register in the green ledger lie on the desk, I hear a muffled knock that rattles the loose pane of the door. Behind frosted glass, a shadow ebbs and flows.

"Tell him to come tomorrow! We're closing. Go on, tell him. What's wrong with these people?"

But after the inner door has shut and no commandments issue from the walls, he pushes into the office: a man in a patched gray suit, testing the carpet with his shoe, twitching like a mole exposed to sunlight, stammering his name. An invisible hammer keeps tapping in his raised hand.

"I had to leave because, you see, because I do not, not belong anymore, because I do not believe." He steadies a finger on his wrist, pointing at a set of blue numerals underlined with a red slash. "I am tired, so many forms to fill out, so many times I am tired, must sign my name, so many times— Listen. Can they hear us? Listen. There are still, you know, still Nazis. It is true. Believe me. Quiet."

He stands up, turns, and fumbles with the door knob, unable to shake it open until suddenly, with a jerk, it pushes him back like the butt of a slapstick routine. He staggers but catches his balance, tugs at his jacket and steps out, closing the door carefully.

45.

The freight express on the mainline
rattles my attic room. Dogs yelp,
a tank rumbles by on maneuvers:
the music of the future.

When the mail scoots under my door
I fret about letter bombs. My landlady
grew up in the States, where she claims
her father was an ambassador.

I walk past the gardens on my way to work,
past the splattered cabbages,
and the shacks with white lace curtains,
and the shingles weighted down with flat stones.

In English as broken as my German,
a refugee tells me of the fountain downtown
where the water flows from bare breasts.
I tell him it's the Fountain of Virtues, but he laughs.

Around the agency building
ragtag groups assemble, unable to converse,
fleeing from nothing to nothing.
What future? What music?

46.

I'm appalled to admire
what was Hitler's favorite opera.

When Hans Sachs, the shoemaker, exhorts
the townsfolk to "honor your German masters,"

I want to say "Careful,"
but the orchestra swells, the chorus

of apprentices crowns Hans
with the poet's laurel.

I like to imagine him
straddling his bench in the moonlight,

insomniac, tapping out beats
on strips of tanned leather.

He shakes his head at the folly,
vowing to give up words for the blows

of his hammer. But then he relents.
The mildness of midsummer night

and the rhythm of his tapping
restore the true masters: Goethe, Bach.

A canticle of love,
a psalm for the dead and the dying.

47.

A drizzle shines the roof tiles, polishes cobblestones. And so, even in the gloom of gray stucco and an overcast sky, when the light's boarded up, something is luminous. Ivy streaks up the corner of a tavern: a string of green bottles glittering in lamplight.

Even the sopping canopies of the marketplace and the puddles reflecting green cupolas of the police station seem grateful, resplendent, burnished from inside. Even the rotting wood of the half-timbered gables and the new, unpainted bolsters shoring up a reconstructed wall seem perfect, though the forecast remains gloomy, more of the same, and the elements have their own explosives. But the faces under scarves and homburgs and watch caps and folded tabloids glow through the dour expressions, through the glowering brows. In spite of everything, even the blank eyes begin to give back light.

48.

On a holiday I walk uphill
toward the refugee camp, the *Lager*,
strolling by the garden plots alongside the path.
As I near the summit, three children
leap from their bikes
jeering *lager! lager! lager! lager!*
in machine gun bursts, dancing
around me in a circle
and chanting their insult:
I belong in the camp, among those who don't belong.

I should tell them
there's a music for the lost, a song
that cannot be stifled, celebrating those who are.
It sounds like jangling, scraping,
a hacksaw through metal. But still
it's a song, and its dissonance is lovely.
It belies the second-hand clothing
and the stubbly beards and the stumbling.
Through the jeers, the noise of machinery, the silence,
an anthem makes itself heard.

Crossing the Border

A la fin tu es las de ce monde ancien
—Apollinaire

It's not just a refugee who tunnels to daylight, gouging
    with a stolen trowel,
not just an orchestra ushered through customs, cellos
    and bassoons checked for contraband,
not just a trucker, coffee cup in hand, whose express-
    way changes from asphalt to dirt ruts.

It's not just a chalk mark, scratched in the street as a
    warning
when you hop off the bus and enter a precinct of
    knives and tattoos,
fires in the trash bins and hydrants cascading.

Move along, the cop drawls, and I take his word for
    necessity,
turning at the newsstand corner, branching off from
    the kiosk,
striding until the highway rims a forest, painted flags
    on the trees,
pacing until traffic grows sparse, except for an
    occasional half-track of infantry.

Crossing a new canal, still closed to barges, smooth
    gravel angled on the sides,
I watch my shadow lurch on sluggish water.
The bank opposing me looks foreign, like an
    unexpected province.

Imagining the check-point, sentries on alert, the
    barriers of customs,
I stall to a halt and the landscape opens—
brambles by the power plant, flagged grasses bursting
    through an air strip,
and, overhead, the zone of frazzled light.

For some who flee, the transition is easy: tickets and a
    forged identity card,
foreign currency in a money belt, an advanced degree
    in obstetrics.

For others, it offers the improbable drama
of curling up in the trunk of a car, or swimming the
    canal at midnight.
The prima ballerina, admitted to an embassy, refuses
    to budge;
the security officer barters away his code book and
    specifications;
the armed guard strolls through a minefield; the
    designer crash-lands in a haystack.

For me, on my way to work, it's the otherwise usual
    morning:
sun at the zenith and breezy, the heavens backed
    nevertheless by black crepe—
the way a mirror, full length, floats on a slick of
    aluminum.

Our atmosphere jostles against the dark, expanding
    universe,
clouds confirming my ambivalence: swelling and

breaking up, lightening as they tumble.
Still, the sunlight penetrates, wiggling through the
    gaps of condensation,
unearthing amphitheaters in the shells of burned-out
    tenements,
replenishing, in a pushcart, the holy-water font of a
    split melon.

Boundaries crosshatch our city—in the broken line of
    a highway
and the roped-off murder scene, the business districts
    and the purlieus,
cracks in the sidewalk, scaffolding, joists, dividers in
    an office,
wards and isolation cells, chains of command, family
    trees.

The headlines of passage, roadblocks, a history of
    crashes and deliverance,
could make the presses run forever, the announcers go
    hoarse with their singing:

news of free clothing in a chain store, gas leaks in the
    infirmary,
news of a submarine, caught on a reef, near a beach of
    sperm whales,
news of revelers and rioters, choiring picket lines,
    bodies on a conveyor belt,
news of migrations, the caravans of nomads, junk in
    the bloodstream,
news of childbirth in a lift and heart attacks at the
    amusement park,

news of commuters playing cards on a briefcase,
    drinking from hip-flasks.

The final edition is never definitive, never more than a
    futile restraining order
when something happens and must be aired, or
    nothing happens and must be passed along,

when whatever emerges goes too far, crosses over,
    breaches, encroaches.
It's not just the scientist, firing enzymes to break
    strands of DNA,
not just the public servant in a dream, lifting the
    automatic from its velvet case,
not just the novice in the wilderness, rappelling down
    an escarpment,
not just the cross-country runner who loses her way
    and comes to a dark estate,
not just the shrimpboat captain who steers, illicit
    nights, close to the rocky coast.

The warrior sticks out his tongue for the hot blade to
    touch:
tested for honesty, he's saved by a layer of saliva as he
    holds his ground.
Buster Keaton dives from a boulder into sand
that, a moment ago, was the sea—and moments
    before that
was the film he drowsed into, leaping from the
    projection booth.

In sleep, the footing is icy. I wait, at night,

in deep woods, watching the headlights of trucks,
    unsure whether to call or stay hidden.
The wind is no comfort. Trees clench their fists. Lights dart
    and leap, thrusting their foils.

And what's on the other side? What demarcations in
    the glare of morning?
Subdivisions, half-acre lots, bus lines, mail routes,
a congregation of beasts in the Peaceable Kingdom,
burial plots, the worn, worried paths of ghosts,
    parading children in Halloween masks,
oxygen tent, diving bell, stake-out around a safe house,
epicenter, ring of official bunkers, sweep on a radar
    screen,
polished cases of stuffed, extinct pigeons,
vicinities of loose bricks, boarded windows, X's on
    doors—

the same doors a freezing woman might jimmy,
the windows a pack of boys might break through,
    exploring and reclaiming,
the pigeons that flew so thick, within the last century,
pioneers trapped them with nets, a dozen fell with one
    round of scattershot.

From the railing above the canal, my shadow on the
    water
shivers and disintegrates, pulls itself together
only to keep on shaking, a fluid collage, mimicking
    me in flashes:
news of impermanence, the dying of news, the demise
    of everything,

news of electrons rallying, light that breaks through
    the chaos of inception.

It's not just myself, or someone I'm afraid I'll lose
to the forte of a slamming door or the lifting of earth
    on a shovel,
not just the criminologist, eager to test out a heist,
not just the homeless man at the terminal, not just the
    traveler who enters a smoky compartment,
not just the waitress, keys in hand after work,
    watching for snipers in the hedges.

We cross the border every time an alarm goes off,
    whenever we wake to a swell of curtains,
each moment we recoil to the smack of weather and
    the pinch of savored taste.

Who chooses to stay on the edge? Who has any choice?
Though the street curb's not much of a precipice, dusk
    is the heaviest door
to prop open, the daylight tugged by a gravity we'd
    never suspect.
On a walk from the office, I'm astounded—
emptied of cars and wagons, the parking lot shines
    like a lagoon,
and the bare, nondescript warehouse looms like a
    palace.

It's not just a girl peeling off torn fishnet stockings,
    mending them like an old salt,
not just the legless bettor on a board with wheels at
    the racetrack,

not just commuters when the subway whines through
   stations
and zooms to the curious boroughs, where they rise to
   a street of blazing storefronts,
not just the news vendors and laid-off typists, the
   bureaucrats and the tramps,
but everyone who opens in surprise at the shifting
   world.

Every cul-de-sac is a port of entry—
and if we look close enough at the crumbling bricks
   and the flaky mortar
and the tatters of posters on billboards and facades,
they are frescoes, inklings of renaissance in the
   shadow's tilt.
Like anything given a close look, they welcome the
   traveler, the exile,
and offer refuge, though their asylum is lighter than
   the wind, hardly a breath,
and the border, where someone might fire a warning
   shot, disappears in long grasses.

Notes

Dedication page: In Dante's *Inferno* (II, 72), Beatrice says to Virgil, "Love moved me and makes me speak" (translated by John D. Sinclair).

Epigraphs: "Der Radwechsel" is reprinted from *Die Gedichte* (2007), Jan Knopf, ed., by permission of Suhrkamp Verlag and the heirs of Bertolt Brecht. Here's my translation:

> I sit on the roadside.
> The driver changes the tire.
> I don't like where I'm coming from.
> I don't like where I'm going to.
> Why do I watch the tire changing
> With impatience?

"These strangers, in a foreign world" is reprinted by permission of the publishers and the Trustees of Amherst College from *The Poems of Emily Dickinson*, Thomas H. Johnson, ed., Cambridge, Mass.: The Belknap Press of Harvard University Press, Copyright © 1951, 1955, 1979, 1983 by the President and Fellows of Harvard College.

The line by Yusef Komunyakaa appears in "Jungle Surrender" from *Pleasure Dome: New and Collected Poems*, © 2001 by Yusef Komunyakaa. Reprinted by permission of Wesleyan University Press.

The Refugee Camp:

Several books helped me with the historical details about Nuremberg: Georg Lohner's *Rundwege Nürnberg*, Ursula Pfistermeister's *Nuremberg*, Erich Mulzer's *Nuremberg*, and Eugen Kusch's *Immortal Nuremberg*.

Section 1: "Heathen's Tower" (*Heidenturm*) overlooks the city of Nuremberg from the imperial castle.

Section 2: The "refugee camp where I work" is the West German *Flüchtlingslager* in Zirndorf, a suburb of Nuremberg.

Section 3: St. Sebald (circa 770) is the patron saint of Nuremberg. According to Kusch, the cross of the "Blackeners of God" was made of silver, painted over by order of the town security council, but Lohner asserts it was a "life-size crucifix on the outside of the west end" of the *Sebalduskirche* and was "really made of bronze."

Section 4: The "golden fountain" is the *Schöner Brunnen* in the *Hauptmarkt*, the main marketplace of Nuremberg. The "Meat Bridge" (*Fleischbrücke*), which has a statue of a recumbent ox at one end, crosses the Pegnitz River and leads to the *Hauptmarkt*. The *Heilig Geist Spital*, now a restaurant over the river, was once a hospice for incurable patients.

Section 5: "Frederick Barbarossa" (1122-1190) was the Holy Roman Emperor. The "robber knight" is Eppelein von Gailingen, who was "supposed to have spurred his horse over the wall to escape being hanged. Look at the hoof-marks on the parapet!"

(Lohner). "David, the apprentice" is Hans Sachs's assistant cobbler and voice pupil in Richard Wagner's music drama, *Die Meistersinger von Nürnberg.*

Section 7: "The music of the future" is Wagner's "*Musik der Zukunft.*" The story about Wagner's misadventure in Nuremberg comes from his autobiography, *Mein Leben.* Beckmesser, the town clerk and pedantic Marker (who rates the performances of the other mastersingers), is the comic antagonist in the opera. "The wall / called *Frauentor Mauer*" encloses the red-light district.

Section 9: Hangman's Bridge (*Henkersteg*) crosses the Pegnitz River. St. Sebaldus is a gothic church near the *Hauptmarkt.*

Section 10: The "*Dudelsack* fountain" is located at the *Unschlittplatz,* but the sculpture is a copy; the original casting is displayed in the German National Museum. "Beckmesser's howling" refers to the dreadful song that sets off a riot after Hans Sachs has marked Beckmesser's own compositional errors by pounding nails into the sole of a shoe he's making.

Section 11: "*St. Jerome* and *Melancholia*" are engravings by Albrecht Dürer (1471-1528), a native of Nuremberg. The phrase "ear, ear for the sea-surge" comes from Ezra Pound's Canto II. *Far from the Madding Crowd* is Thomas Hardy's novel about Gabriel Oak, the shepherd, and his love for Bathsheba Everdene.

Section 12: Martin Behaim (1459-1507), who was born in Nuremberg, was a navigator and geographer. Nicolaus Glockenthon (circa 1505) was the artist who drew the maps for Behaim's terrestrial globe.

Section 13: The "German agency" is *das Bundesamt für die Anerkennung ausländischer Flüchtlinge*, the Federal Agency for the Recognition of Foreign Refugees in Zirndorf, West Germany.

Section 17: Adam Kraft (circa 1455-1509) was a sculptor of stone who worked in Nuremberg. The "saint it was carved for" is St. Lawrence, who lived in Rome during the first half of the Third Century and was burned alive on a gridiron.

Section 19: The "American expatriate / singing 'Hallo partner, danke schön'" is Peggy March, whose big hit was "I Will Follow Him." The other song is "Wouldn't It Be Loverly" from Lerner and Loewe's *My Fair Lady*.

Section 21: The "prince of this world," originally located by the Bridal Portal of the *Sebalduskirche*, is a statue carved from sandstone around 1325. Sigismund (1368-1437), Holy Roman Emperor, was born in Nuremberg. Peter Vischer the Elder (circa 1455-1529) was a sculptor and bronze-caster whose self-portrait is part of his shrine to St. Sebald, the "tomb lifted up by carved snails" mentioned in Section 3.

Section 22: "Nuremberg's golden funnel" is the *Nürnberger Trichter*, a comic illustration of teaching by rote, an instructor pouring knowledge into a pupil's brain.

Section 23: Hans Sachs (1494-1576), the real-life Mastersinger, "*Schuhmacher und Poet dazu*," serves as the main character of Wagner's opera.

Section 26: *Triumph of the Will* (1935) is Leni Riefenstahl's propaganda film about the 1934 Nazi Party rally in Nuremberg.

Section 28: Bedrich Smetana (1824-1888) composed *The Moldau*, one of six tone poems that comprise *Má vlast*, a symphonic cycle.

Section 29: Johann Pachelbel (1653-1706), a native of Nuremberg, served as organist of the *Sebalduskirche*. The religion of the "Iranian / whose faith embraces all faiths" is Bahá'í.

Section 35: The "house, baroque and spared from air raids," is the Fembo house, now the city museum of Nuremberg.

Section 37: The "graveyard where Dürer is buried" is the *Johannisfriedhof*, outside the medieval walls of the city.

Section 38: The "church of Our Lady" (*Frauenkirche*) is located in the main marketplace.

Section 39: The "corner stonework" belongs to the *Lorenzkirche*. The Martin Luther chorale is "*Ein' feste Burg ist unser Gott*." Veit Stoss (circa 1450-1533) was a sculptor of wood.

Section 42: In Wagner's *Meistersinger*, the poet is the heroic tenor, Walther von Stolzing, who woos Eva Pogner by means of his prize song and is opposed by the marker Sixtus Beckmesser. Kaspar Hauser (circa 1812-1833) was a mysterious teenager who turned up in Nuremberg one day, possibly an impostor, telling different stories about being raised in the wild or imprisoned in a cell, bearing two letters of introduction he may have written himself; a few years later, he died mysteriously in Ansbach, the victim of a knife wound, possibly self-inflicted.

Section 45: The "Fountain of Virtues" (*Tugend-brunnen*) is located by the *Lorenzkirche*.

Section 46: "Honor your German masters" is a translation of "*Ehrt eure deutschen Meister,*" the admonition of Hans Sachs, taken up by the chorus of townspeople in the finale of *Die Meistersinger*. The next line is "*dann bannt ihr gute Geister!*" (meaning "then you will call up good spirits!").

Section 48: *Lager* means "camp" and refers to the refugee camp, made up of dormitories and administration buildings.

Crossing the Border:

Epigraph: Guillaume Apollinaire, "Zone" (line 1), translated by Louis Simpson as "You're weary of this ancient world at last."

The "new canal" (also mentioned in the line "From the railing above the canal, my shadow on the water") is the Rhine-Main-Danube canal, which passes through Nuremberg.

Buster Keaton is the star and director of *Sherlock Jr.*, in which he plays a movie projectionist.

John Drury is the author of two previous full-length poetry collections, *Burning the Aspern Papers* and *The Disappearing Town*, both published by Miami University Press, as well as a chapbook of poems, *The Stray Ghost* (State Street Press). He has also written *The Poetry Dictionary* and *Creating Poetry*, both published by Writer's Digest Books. His awards include a Pushcart Prize, two Ohio Arts Council grants, an Ingram Merrill Foundation fellowship, and the Bernard F. Conners Prize from *The Paris Review*. His poems have appeared in *The American Poetry Review*, *The Hudson Review*, *The New Republic*, *Poetry*, *Shenandoah*, *The Southern Review*, *Western Humanities Review*, and other periodicals. He teaches at the University of Cincinnati.

CPSIA information can be obtained at www.ICGtesting.com
Printed in the USA
BVOW031958260911

272159BV00001B/21/P